Le Père Noël vous remercie
de l'avoir aidé à répondre
à son courrier de 1993.

Thank you for helping Santa
answer his mail in 1993.

Dear Santa
Cher Père Noël

Dear Santa

Children's Letters to the North Pole

Cher Père Noël

Lettres d'enfants transmises au pôle Nord

Random House of Canada / Random House du Canada
Toronto

Published in Canada in 1993 by Random House of Canada Limited, Toronto.
Publié au Canada en 1993 par Random House du Canada limitée (Toronto).

Canadian Cataloguing in Publication Data

Main entry under title:
Dear Santa

Canada Post ed.
Text in English and French.
ISBN 0-394-22399-3

1. Children's writings, Canadian. 2. Children –
Canada – Correspondence. 3. Santa Claus –
Correspondence. I. Canada Post Corporation.

PS8235.C4D4 1993a   C816'.5408'09282   C93-095196-4E
PR9194.5.C5D4 1993a

Données de catalogage avant publication (Canada)

Vedette principale au titre:
Cher Père Noël

Canada Post ed.
Textes en français et en anglais.
ISBN 0-394-22399-3

1. Écrits d'enfants canadiens. 2. Enfants –
Canada – Correspondance. 3. Père Noël –
Correspondance. I. Société canadienne des postes.

PS8235.C4D4 1993a   C816'.5408'09282   C93-095196-4F
PR9194.5.C5D4 1993a

Jacket illustration: Mireille Levert
Design: Teri McMahon

Illustration de la jaquette: Mireille Levert
Conception: Teri McMahon

Printed and bound in Canada
Imprimé et relié au Canada

10 9 8 7 6 5 4 3 2 1
Toronto, New York, London, Sydney, Auckland

MAIL ➤ POSTE

Canada Post Corporation / Société canadienne des postes

The Santa Letter-Writing Program supports literacy by encouraging children to write letters to Santa and by promoting correct addressing and use of the postal code.

In 1992 alone, Canada Post elves helped Santa respond to close to 1 million letters from children across Canada. These elves were rewarded with smiles – smiles on the faces of children from coast to coast who were ecstatic that they received their very own letter from Santa Claus.

As we celebrate the 10th Anniversary of this national program, Canada Post Corporation and Random House of Canada are very pleased to share with you some of their favourite letters. We hope you'll like them too!

In keeping with the spirit of this project, Canada Post Corporation will donate any royalties received from the sale of this book to further the cause of literacy in Canada.

POSTE > MAIL

Société canadienne des postes / Canada Post Corporation

Le Programme de lettres au Père Noël apporte son soutien à l'alphabétisation en incitant les enfants à écrire au Père Noël, ainsi qu'en faisant la promotion de l'exactitude des adresses et de l'utilisation du code postal.

Durant la seule année de 1992, les petits lutins de la Société canadienne des postes ont répondu à près d'un million de lettres d'enfants partout au Canada. Ces petits lutins ont reçu leur récompense en voyant la mine réjouie de ces enfants lisant leur propre lettre du Père Noël.

En ce 10e anniversaire du programme national, la Société canadienne des postes et Random House du Canada sont très heureux de partager avec vous quelques-unes de ses lettres préférées. Nous espérons que vous les aimerez autant que nous!

Fidèle à l'esprit de ce projet, la Société canadienne des postes fera don des droits d'auteur provenant de la vente de ce livre pour appuyer l'alphabétisation au Canada.

Dear Santa

I've Tried Not To Bug My Brother and My Sister. I Tried Not To Bug My MoM and My DaD When They'er Talking With Other people. Now let's get Down To Business! For Christmas I Would like a alarm clock and a few Surprises

oh ya here's a Joke: Why Didn't Rudolph's Nose light up at first Batteries Weren't included.

I Will leave you a ginger BreaD House. Love Kelcey

Kelcey
Brandon, Manitoba

Dear Santa Claus,

My name is Jackie,
I am in grade 2. I am 7 years
old and I love school.
    I've ben sortof good
because I lied and when
I wake my Mom and Dad
up they don't like it. Santa
I'll don't lie anymore
becouse I got grounded once.

I help my Mom with Megan and I can change her diaper. My Mom said I'm good at figureskating but I'm not good at taking out the garbage because it is stinky, but I'm good at playing with my sister.

Mery Christmas!
Love,
Jackie

Jackie
Delta, British Columbia

DEAR SANTA
I AM BEING A GOOD BOY
MY FAVORITE TOYS
ARE CARS TRAINS AND
GAMES

PLEASE BRING ME

SOME SURPRIZES

LOVE

GEOFFREY

Geoffrey
Nepean, Ontario

cher père noël,

bonjour je m'appelle guillaume. j'ai
8 ans. j'aime bien l'école mes amis, et ma
famille. mon papa est transfaré à little
grandrapid. je suis allé le voir. sur l'avion
mon frère a vomit.

guillaume

Guillaume
Elie, Manitoba

dear Santa Clause

How are you doing? And have you had a good year? i was wondering haw old are you and your reindeer? when a reindeer gets old do they get old and retire? or do they go on and on and on for ever and ever?

And how do you get down the chimany. this christmas may you please tell the reindeer to land just a bit harder on the roof so i can hear them. evry christmas i can not hear them when they land on the roof at night.

Michael

Michael
West Vancouver,
British Columbia

dear santa claus,

i have a question, did you really kiss my mom? because it said in a song called, "i saw santa kiss mommy." but, i don't think your that rude! Like, i mean, your already married! i hope that you have merry christmas.

thank you, devon

p.s. please, please, please write back, and remember to wear a scarf because it's very chilly outside.

Devon
Lundar, Manitoba

Dear Santa Claus,
I don't want anything for Xmas. I have everything I want my brother and mom.

I guess I've finally gotten into the Christmas spirit. What is the Christmas spirit really? It's about giving something special to those with nothing, seeing smiles on needy children and putting all wars on halt this month. It's about accepting people as they are with, no matter how rich or poor they are.

Merry Christmas
Your Friend Heather-May

Heather-May
Peterborough, Ontario

dear santa,

i am 4 years old. i love you very much. i live on the mirimichi river. you should come and fish with me in the summertime. my daddy is a fireman and keeps the flu clean so you can come down it on christmas night.

Erin

Erin
Doaktown, New Brunswick

Dear Santa
My name is Sean. I am 7 years old. your hat got stuck in our chimney last year. It will Be By the cookees that steven, my little Brother, and I will leave for you. Can you please Bring me some cind of lego for christmas. thank you for cuming to our house.

Love Sean

Sean
Winnipeg, Manitoba

dear santa,

this year i do not have a list of presents or anything like that. all i want is
for everyone to have every thing they
need. sutch as food, shelter and peace in
ther countrys. i am one of the more
forchunat people. santa please help the
people that need help. this year my new
year resuluchon is to give more than i
receve. well good bye, write back soon.

véronique

**Véronique
Orleans, Ontario**

Dearest: Santa Claus, I am writing this letter to you all by myself, with a little help from my sister. How are you and Mrs. Claus doing, and we can not forget the elves and Rudolf and the other reindeers, can we? As for me I'm doing fine. I can't wait for Christmas to come. I am so excited. This year I think I've been pretty good. I've made alot of new freinds in grade one and at recess we like to tell each other what we hope to get for Christmas. Anyway This year I would like Rollerblade Xbarbie, baby Rollerblade and beach waterbaby. please don't forget my friends in Riverview, an all the people who have to be in jail or the hospital for Christmas or the poor people. I know that you

won't you've never let me down, Santa, and I know you never will. I love you Santa. I won't forget to leave out your favorite cookies with your milk

love Amanda

P.S. Would you like your milk warmed up

P.S.S please Santa, Don't forget to write me, I Believe in you.

**Amanda
Riverview,
New Brunswick**

dear santa,

How are ya? i am 8 Years old. How old are you? i Have been good. (Sorta.) How is Mrs. clause? MY Sister AshLeY, is Mrs. clause in Her play. it's about Santa who Has to Loose Lots of weight. (No afence.) i am going to be the Mother bell in MY play. it's called. the Little bell that could Not ring. the plays are for our Christmas consert. oH ya. what i want for christmas: a road race track, (my dad wants it more.) and, that's all i can think of so . . . one more thing. an old lady named grandma zoody died so i am sad. oh ya, i also want walkie-talkie.

Love karley

Karley
Winnipeg, Manitoba

dear santa,

How are you doing? i'm doing
fine.
i want to be your penpal but i
think you are too busy. i have a crush
on John and He likes me i know that
because He always went after me in
the game Hugtag. because you have to
Hug the person. He always Hugged me.

when our class played chain saw He always Hold my Hand. but John actually kissed me on the Lips when we were playing kiss your partner. you Have to kiss your partner for 20 seconds. it was gross. i don't know what to do? please write back!

your friend, Alison

Alison
Vancouver,
British Columbia

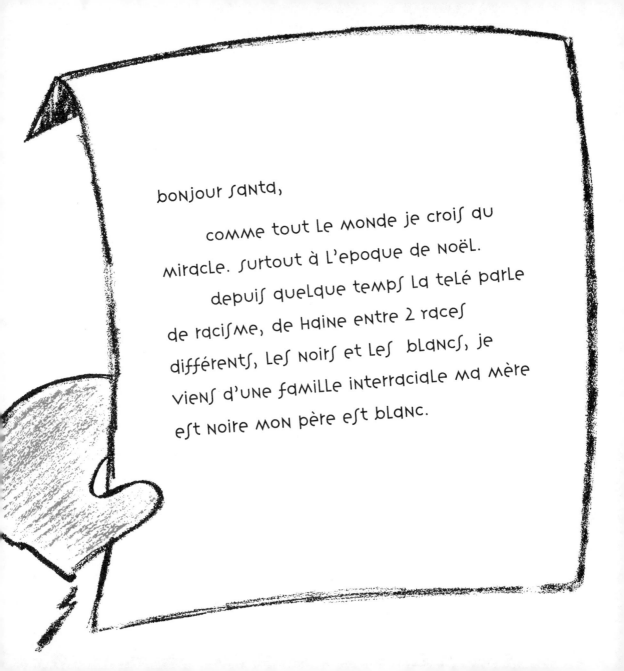

bonjour santa,

comme tout le monde je crois au miracle. surtout à l'epoque de noël.

depuis quelque temps la telé parle de racisme, de haine entre 2 races différents, les noirs et les blancs, je viens d'une famille interraciale ma mère est noire mon père est blanc.

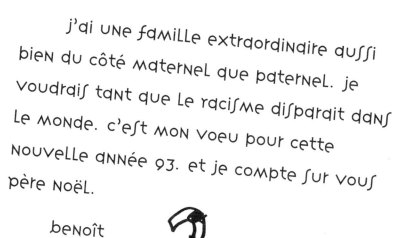

j'ai une famille extraordinaire aussi bien du côté maternel que paternel. je voudrais tant que le racisme disparait dans le monde. c'est mon voeu pour cette nouvelle année 93. et je compte sur vous père noël.

benoît

**Benoît
Ottawa, Ontario**

Dear Santa Claus.

How are you? Well I am fine.

I only want four things for
Christmas.
Clothes, Barbies, love, and to see my dad.

Oh how is miss claus? I sure hope she's
well.
        Mery Christmas.

        Love, Jamie-Lee

**Jamie-Lee
Winnipeg, Manitoba**

Dear Santa Claus, I've always wanted to know how do you finish, well not always finish, but eat all the food people leave you? I'm sure you get a wide varity of food, because you go all the way around the world. Is it true you use lateries to run your sled? I don't think so. Your sleigh is magic Cause on this comircial I saw you (well not you a imitation) using lateries to power the sleigh I guess it was just to promote the latterie. Does it get really cold up in the North pole? like -50 celeus. I got that cold here once, but just vonce, as far vas I've been alive.

From, ♥
Kristen

Kristen
Lively, Ontario

DEAR SANTA,

I am doing very good in school. On my last test I got 32 out of 32. I only would like a few things............................ a cemestry set + two game boy games.

THANK-YOU VERY MUCH!

P.S. HAVE A SAFE RIDE HOME and BE POWER SMART.

FROM,

Matthew

Matthew
Brandon, Manitoba

Bonjour pere—Noël et men-
Noël! J'ai bien hâte
à Noël. J'ai eu un nou-
veau petit frère, et il nou-
lest formidable. J'espère
que tu vas lui apporter
beaucoup de cadeaux.

Ne t'inquiète pas Samuel
est très sage, Marie-Pier
et samuel. xxx

**Marie-Pier
et Samuel
Gatineau, Québec**

Dear Santa;

My name is Brent.
I am 7 years old and in grade 2. I try to be good but bad slips out sometimes. But I am good most of the time. Why are you so nice? I Love my mom, DAD + Sister. For christmas I want a nintendo Baseball game. skates and Army men and A game for my sister. O:K DoH't forget IF you caint its to give presents to the poor people.

Love Brent.

**Brent
Scarborough, Ontario**

Dear santa claus

My christmas wish is for a clean world with no more garbage and no drugs and no smoking. I would like a Ninja Turtle for christmas.

Love

DeNNis

Dennis
Wanipigow, Manitoba

Dear Santa:

Its been a long time that my mother wrote you a letter to you when she was a little girl. a want you to help her to find her real mother. It would be nice for a Christmas present. Her name (mother) is Madeleine

Yours truly, Mélanie
with all my
love...

[Note: This wish came true soon after, with the help of an organization that links birth mothers and their children.]

**Mélanie
Gloucester, Ontario**

Dear Santa

For this christmas all I want is to have a interview with you. And I also want a interview with Rudolph one day before christmas please. I'm afraid that if you do not come with Rudolph I may never believe agian.

P.S May I have you'r autograph and Rudolph's hoof print in ink.

Kimberley

Kimberley
Don Mills, Ontario

Dear Santa

My name is Chad. Just in case
you get lost my numbers
in the book.
I've tried to be very good
this year. Hows your wife
and the deer. Say Hi from their
pal.
I'm going to leave you some milk
and Cookies.

For Christmas I
would like:

1) Some Clothes
2) a TV
3) a bean bag chair
4) a Nintendo game
5) my dad to be home. One
   big happy Family
When you come I will be
fast asleep thinking of sugar
plumbs and candy canes dancing
in my head

Chad

PS:
My Friends
dont Believe
But I Do

Chad
Winnipeg, Manitoba

Dear; Santa I have
Being triing to be
good I just can't control
my temper; For cristmas
I want a remote central
F-14 tomcat here is
a picture of it so
your elves can
make it;

from; Butch

Butch
Millbank, Ontario

Dear old santa,
My name is Gina Mertikas. For Christmas I would
kindly aprichiate it if you gave my a puppy. If poseble a Golden Retriver.
I don't mind what kind. I would really love a puppy for Christmas.
I'll give you milk and cookies. What do you want milk and cookies, or
carrot stics and juice? Say hi to Rudolf and the other reindeer for me.
Don't forget the puppy. If you can't get me a puppy a computer if poseble.
I'd really like a puppy though. All my friends have a animal. So please a
A puppy. (computer) .
I love you.

P.s. Don't forget to write
back.(a puppy or a
computer)

From Gina

Gina
Ottawa, Ontario

Dear Santa

For Christmas I Would like
3 things from you.

I Would like Master Work Shop.

I Would like roller blades,

my Cousin jeffry is sick, with your
miracles please make him better.

Luke

Luke
Nepean, Ontario

Cher père et mère noël !
Je vais te faire un poème

Le Père-Noël,
Lance des bibelle
Plein le ciel.
Avant la messe,
On fait une cieste
Quand on réveillonne,
On mange des tourtières très bonnes.
L'été je me rappelle de l'hiver,
Comme si c'était hier.

Je te laisserai une brioche
et un verre de lait sur la table.

Maxime

Maxime
Malartic, Québec

Dear Santa,

I want world peace and the hunger problem solved. Maybe you can throw tons of food down from the sky in places like Ethiopia or something.

From
Kit

Kit
Inwood, Manitoba

Dear Santa

I have been a good girl, I wear underwear now!

For christmas I would like a cradle for my dolls and maybe some new underwear.

Love,

Olivia

Olivia
Ottawa, Ontario

Dear Santa,

Hi this Kelsey. I'm from Halifax Nova Scotia.
I went to Cambridge for a year so my mom
could go to Harvard. She's 40 now. It was
two years ago. For christmas I don't need
something too good just a little something
like pencils that have all kinds of colours
on them and stickers. Well are the
reindeer almost ready? Please write back
before Christmas I love reading your
letters. It's fun. I have a guinea pig
named Snuggles She isn't a ordinary

guinea pig she isn't scared of anything.
She expresses her feelings. Like when
I was little I brought her too
school and when I was talking about
her she looked back with expression
that says "HOW COULD YOU DO THIS
TO ME!!!

Yours Truly

Kelsey

Kelsey
Halifax, Nova Scotia

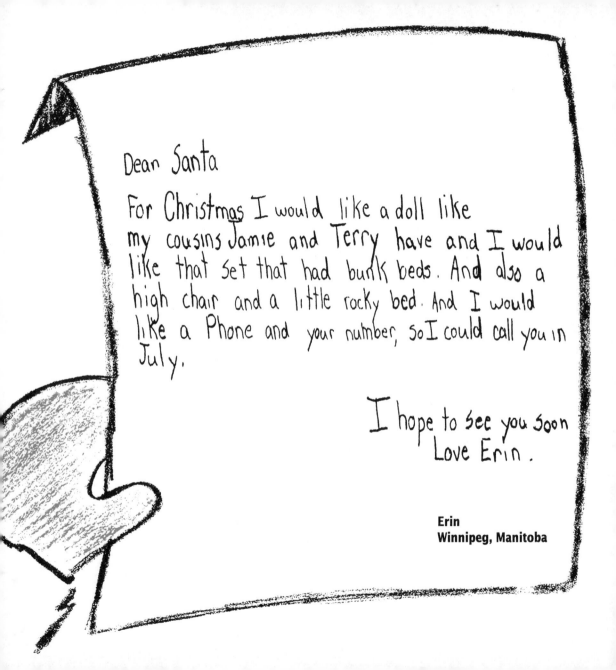

Dear Santa

For Christmas I would like a doll like
my cousins Jamie and Terry have and I would
like that set that had bunk beds. And also a
high chair and a little rocky bed. And I would
like a Phone and your number, so I could call you in
July.

I hope to see you soon
Love Erin.

Erin
Winnipeg, Manitoba

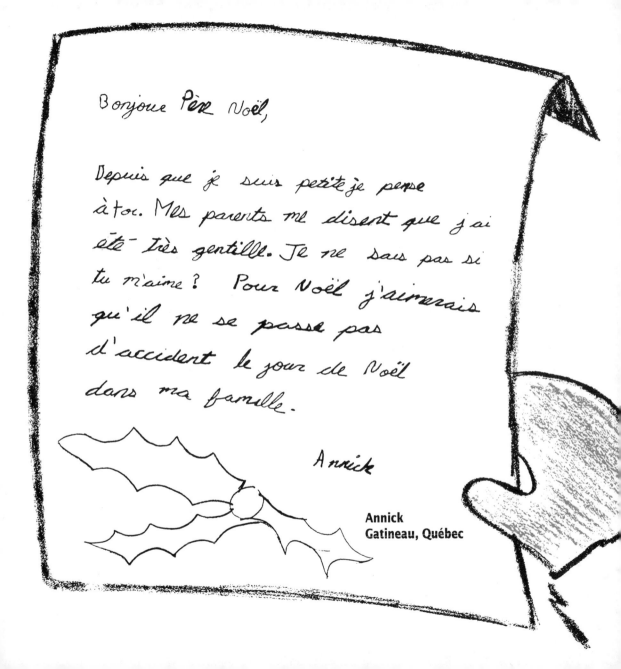

Bonjour Père Noël,

Depuis que je suis petite je pense à toi. Mes parents me disent que j'ai été très gentille. Je ne sais pas si tu m'aime? Pour Noël j'aimerais qu'il ne se passe pas d'accident le jour de Noël dans ma famille.

Annick

**Annick
Gatineau, Québec**

Dear Santa,

My name is Cung. I am 10 years old How's it going in the North Pole? I am really looking forward to Christmas this year. On December 24th my mom is going to visit Cambodia (that's where my grandma lives) so I am going to be very lonely, that's why I really want you to come to my house and give me presents. If you come I will be very happy. My brother Meng will be happy too. His is 8 years old. I won't be having a christmas party or tree this year because my mom is not going to be at the party anyways.

This is a picture of a flower called "Pointsetta"
It is looking out the window!

From: Cung

Cung
Vancouver,
British Columbia

dear santa claus,

     i am in the 5th grade and i like swim-
ming and skate-boarding. my name is
eugin. i migrated from malaysia in
september, so i am new to this country. i
hope to be a lawyer in 14 years.
     i was wondering if i could ask you
some questions, like:
1. How cold is the temperature in the north
pole?
2. How did rudolph get a red nose?

3. does the sun really turn green in the north pole? (i read it somewhere.)

for christmas i would like the world to have peace and vancouver to have the greatest peace of all. i would like to have a v.c.r. for christmas. well goodbye!

yours truly, eugin

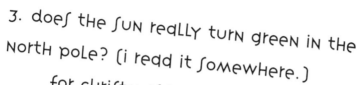

**Eugin
North Vancouver,
British Columbia**

Dear Santa. I really, really would appreciate it if you would bring me the most biggest stuffed animal you can find and I was wondering if you could bring a little something for my two favorite stuffed animals Blossom and Spot. There will be a chocolate chip cookie and maybe something else,

yours truely
Jennifer

I love you with all
heart and I belive in
you very, very much.

Y O Y O X O XO

Jennifer
Kanata, Ontario

dear ∫aNta

Here'∫ a pome for you ∫aNta
i wi∫H a Little cHild Like me, could ∫omeHow
cHaNge thi∫ world i ∫ee. i wi∫H that i could
∫top tHe Hate aNd eNd tHe war∫ tHat meN
create. i wi∫H tHat i could uNder∫taNd wHy
cHildreN iN ∫o maNy LaNd∫ wiLL Never Have a
cHaNce of LiviNg free, Like You aNd me.

i wish that we could find a way to feed the hungry every day. i wish we all could find the love to do the things i'm thinking of and that's the way i wish the world could be for you and me.

SHAWN

**Shawn
Burnaby,
British Columbia**

Dear Santa Claus
I wanted to ask you for a pair of ice skates but what
I really want for Christmas is to have a very happy year of
nineteen ninety-three. What I mean is peace on earth and
no wars for a few years.

Merry Christmas
From your friend
Natalie

Natalie
Winnipeg, Manitoba

Bonjour mon Beau père Noël D'amour
Je sais que tu Reçoit plusieurs lettres
comme celle-ci mais s.v.p prend compte
de la mienne.

Premièrement j'espère que tu vas bien,
Parce que moi je vais à merveille! J'aimerais
avoir un lit à deux étages pour poupée mais
ce que je désirerais le plus chèrement c'est
que tout les petits enfants du monde mangent
à leur faim le jour de Noël.

s.v.p fait de ton mieux. J'ai été très
gentille durant l'année 1992. merci beaucoup
d'avance. À l'an prochain. répond-moi vite.

Je T'aime

XXX

d'une petite fille de 7 ans.

Julie

Julie
Maskinongé, Québec

Dear Santa Claus .

For Cnristmas I would like a fancy party dress and Roller
    Blade barbie . I hope you will have time to write to me back
because I love getting letters from you . I still have the letter
    you sent me last year . You may recognize my name because I
sent you a letter that we made in school it is all about what I want
    you to give people that do not have money . I wish I could see
    you but I am never awake at midnight . If you want to see my
    room it is the second room upstairs .

                    Love
                        Jenny

THIS IS YOU SANTA

Jenny
Surrey,
British Columbia

Dear santa and elves and raindeers, I hope you have some good presents for me and last year you gave me a baisball mitt and I really needed one because I lost

my other mitt I want
to thank you for giveing
it to me because thats
what friends are for

Thank you !!!
love George. I love
you santa

**George
New Westminster,
British Columbia**

Dear Santa,

This is Karl. in case you
don't know. I have been medyocor
acording to my parents. It's because
Anna gets me in trouble. Anyways heres
a list of the top Ten things I would
like.

1. — A Telescope
2. — T.V. or telephone
3. — A monster face
4. — an Art drawing board
5. — A paire of roler blades.

6. – A book
7. – Nicnacks that you always bring.
8. – Legos
9. – more Legos
10. – Super Nintendo or (Game boy)

P.S. You might not be able to bring me all of them but you tried.
P.P.S.
Just bring one or two

Karl
Aylmer, Québec

Dear & Santa Claus,

Hi!

For
Christmas I would like the world to never have a war again and I wish Vancovver snows enough to not go to school and for chrismas I would like toys.

your Friend
Nikki

Nikki
North Vancouver,
British Columbia

Dear Santa,

Hello! How are things in the North Pole? I bet its brrrr..... cold. Well, how is Mrs. Claus? And the elves? I don't mean to sound pushy but for christmas I wouldn't mind a computer. Or a pair of Guess Jeans That's all really. Well, I better go.

WBS (Write Back Soon)

From,

Alison

P.P.S. WE DO NOT HAVE A CHIMNEY!
HO HO HO

Alison
Winnipeg, Manitoba

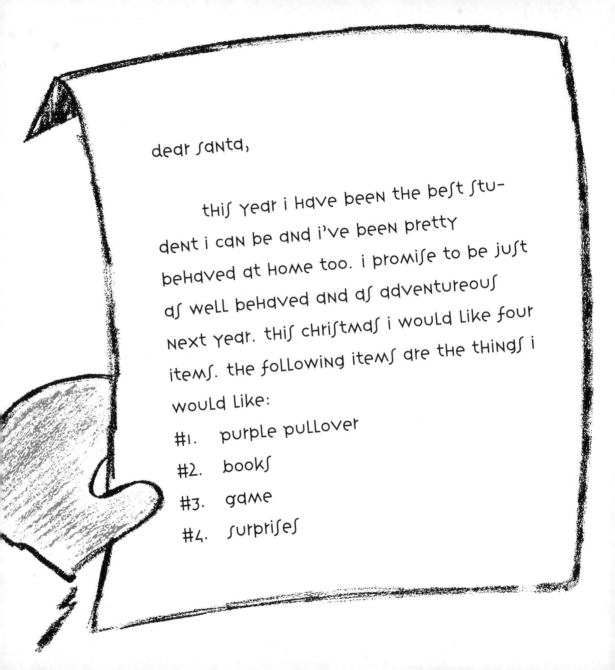

dear santa,

        this year i have been the best stu-
dent i can be and i've been pretty
behaved at home too. i promise to be just
as well behaved and as adventureous
next year. this christmas i would like four
items. the following items are the things i
would like:

#1.   purple pullover

#2.   books

#3.   game

#4.   surprises

i would really like items 1 and 4. i hope its dry on christmas night so you don't get all wet.

sincerely yours, heather

p.s. we have a gas fire.
How are you going to get in?

Heather
Coquitlam,
British Columbia

Dear Santa,

How was youre Summer. Mine was really good. The only thing I want is my Grandmother to get better. She fell in are van. She went to hospital today. My Grandad is blind. and can't help. her. He was a nice man. He told us stories and they were good. If you have time I could do with a troll, black jeans, A Nintendo game (Contra), A wrestling dummy, some hockey cards, A tape of the Beach boys Christmas tape, A Chichgo Bulls jaket, A Gameboy. And please make it snow on Christmas.

If you can't do it money will be fine
tens and twenties is what I could have.
One more thing is a pear of black hitops.

Youre pal Timothy

JOLLY
SANTALO
CLAUS!

**Timothy
Richmond,
British Columbia**

cher Père Noël

Bomjour coment sa va?

Sa va bien ici.

Je veux des chacolats pour Noël.

Je sais tu as beaucoup de magique.

Est-ce-que tu peux regarder mon
jeu de Hockey le vingt-neuf decembre

Je veux pas de cadeaux pour
Noël je veux des amis, d'amour,

Mais si tu as le temps tu peux
donner des cadeau.

XoXoXoXoXoXOxOxOxO

DE BRETT

Brett
Ste-Rose, Manitoba

Dear santa claus. Some of my friends do not bileve in you. But I do, and for Cristmas I would like to get princess Ariel, totally hair barbie, Pritty Crimp'n Curl, princess Copier, take-parfaits, magic Jewels, Magic Copier, take-along copier, Barbie Fold and Fun house, Grape Escapes, Giggle Wiggle, tornado Rex, Perfection, Gone fishin'and Scale Electric train set. if you cant bring all of it, and can't make all of it just please give me just some of them for cristmas. And don't forget I do bileave in-you. and I always did, and I still do, forever. (and please help me to not suck my thumb.)

I am
7 year's
old

From Jodie

Jodie
Kamloops,
British Columbia

Dear Santa Claus,

How are you? I am fine, I am 7 years old now but I will be 8 soon. Mom and Dad say I am a good girl. This year I hope there is enough toys for all The poor boys and girls, if there is not enough toys then could you please bring them some food, if I am old enough could you please bring me a walkman, if not Then could you bring me a Barbie or just a surprise.

Thank you Santa,

Love Kristal

Kristal
Pipestone, Manitoba

Bonjour,

je m'appele Simon et j'ai 4 ans. je t'en voie ma liste de cadeaux. quelques fois je suis tannant mais je vais etres plus sage a l'avenir. L'autre jour je t'ai vu arriver du pole nord. j'ai passé une jour née fantastique: ce que j'aime le plus ce sont les autos.

Simon

Simon
Aylmer, Québec

Dear Santa Claus,
Christmas is nice!
Hear the bells a-ring-a-ting-ting,
Rest in Peace and always love,
I like Christmas it is the best,
Stop and care for other people,
Take someone shopping make it good,
Make someone happy make them feel good
Always care and love I say
Steel never, care is the thing,

            Love   Todd

There will be a present for you
by your stuff,

**Todd
Aldergrove,
British Columbia**

Ho! Ho! Ho!

À père Noël

Je m'appelle Andréanne. J'ai 6 ans.

J'aimerais avoir un beau cadeau
pour moi et aussi que tu en
donnes aux petits enfants pauvres
Je t'aime beaucoup

de Andréanne

X X X X
X X X
X X X X
X X X X

**Andréanne
La Présentation,
Québec**

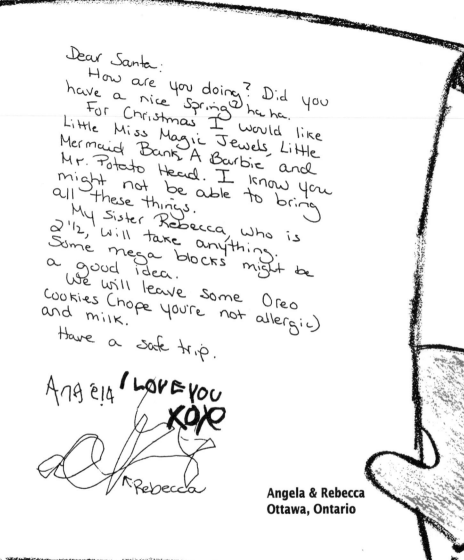

Dear Santa:
How are you doing? Did you
have a nice spring? ha ha.
For Christmas I would like
Little Miss Magic Jewels, Little
Mermaid Bank, A Barbie and
Mr. Potato Head. I know you
might not be able to bring
all these things.
My sister Rebecca, who is
2 1/2, will take anything.
Some mega blocks might be
a good idea.
We will leave some Oreo
cookies (hope you're not allergic)
and milk.
Have a safe trip.

Angela I LOVE YOU
XOXO
Rebecca

Angela & Rebecca
Ottawa, Ontario

Dear: Santa Merry chrisTMas and
Happy New Year. I want for christ
as a telescope and chess
Game and that all the poor people
have a very Merry christMas and get
food, and Peace on earth and
No Body get hurt. I am 9 years
old

yours truly Jim

**Jim
Lucan, Ontario**

Dear Santa Claus how are you? Fine I hope.
for christmas I want lots of surprises please.
Say hi to rudolph and the other reindeers.
And say hi to mrs. Claus please. I have been a good girl.
I have a new cat, Frekles she would like a
present too please. Be care full not to step on her
tail on christmas Eve.

Love
Crystal

Crystal
Moncton,
New Brunswick

Dear Santa,

I hope this wish will come true. Can you please help my cousin Perry because he was one of my best cousins. He went out on his ski-doo one day and hit a tree. Now he is in acoma. Please let this wish come true. I'm sorry I can't write any more sad things because I will start to cry. But just please help the people that are like Perry and that have other problems and diseases. Thank you for all of the time you take for everybody and thank you for my presents every year.

Your Friend,
Amber

Amber
Brandon, Manitoba

dear santa

i don't need anything for xmas. if you have any extra money, please give it to the prime-minister so he can buy something for his family. my parents told me that he is out of money and that canada has a big dificit.

yours truly, butchie

Butchie
Winnipeg, Manitoba

Dear Santa Claus,

Santa I want you to give me a sega Genesis.
Santa, how come you bring presents in the night?
I want a stereo, a t.v a phone and a
million$! Where did you go to university?
Santa, did you watch the grey cup

Sincirely,
Justin

P.S. ask mrs, claus to bake me
a cake!

Justin
Winnipeg, Manitoba

Dear Santa,
I'm very sorry that
I'm late writing your
letter. It's just that I
couldn't make up my
mind what I wanted.
But since I thought
a computer was to much
I decided to ask you
for a typewriter if you
have any made.
Thank you
Very Much
please write back!
love. Courtney

Courtney
Charlottetown,
Prince Edward Island

Dear Santa,
I wrote this poem for you, And I wanted
to tell you I want a suprize for
Christmas.

Christmas day
The stockings were packed with presen
to you see,
And one of the presents was made just
for me.

But then I heard a jingle far far away,
I looked out the window and saw Santas sleigh.
And then I woke up and new I was dreaming
And I new Christmas day was begining!

The End
Mitchell

Mitchell
Carberry, Manitoba

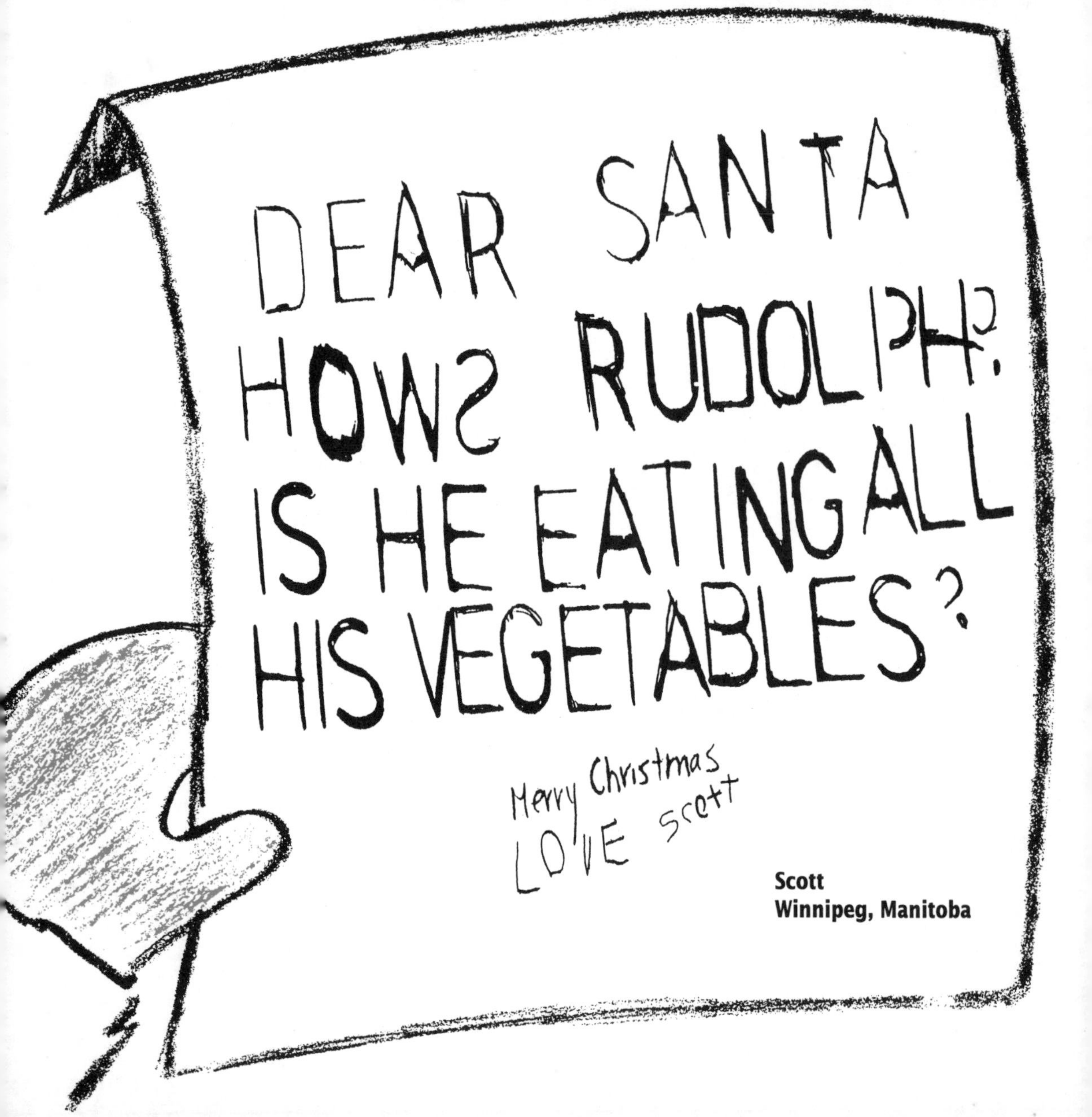

Scott
Winnipeg, Manitoba